BARBERS

CHRISTINE HONDERS

PowerKiDS press™

New York

Published in 2020 by The Rosen Publishing Group, Inc.
29 East 21st Street, New York, NY 10010

First Edition

Editor: Greg Roza
Book Design: Reann Nye

Photo Credits: Cover, p.1 Odua Images/Shutterstock.com; pp. 4–22 Abstractor/Shutterstock.com; p. 5 Aksinia Abiagam/Shutterstock.com; p. 7 Juan Marmolejos/Shutterstock.com; p. 9 https://commons.wikimedia.org/wiki/File:A_barber-surgeon_extracting_stones_from_a_woman%27s_head;_symb_Wellcome_V0016251.jpg; p. 11 bodytaylor/Shutterstock.com; p. 13 F8 studio/Shutterstock.com; p. 15 Thomas Barwick/DigitalVision/Getty Images; p. 17 JHU Sheridan Libraries/Gado/Archive Photos/Getty Images; p. 19 Jetta Productions Inc/DigitalVision/Getty Images; p. 21 fizkes/Shutterstock.com; p. 22 Mike Harrington/DigitalVision/Getty Images.

Library of Congress Cataloging-in-Publication Data

Names: Honders, Christine, author.
Title: Barbers / Christine Honders.
Description: New York : PowerKids Press, [2020] | Series: Helpers in our
  community | Includes index.
Identifiers: LCCN 2019009057| ISBN 9781725308060 (pbk.) | ISBN 9781725308084
  (library bound) | ISBN 9781725308077 (6 pack)
Subjects: LCSH: Barbers–History–Juvenile literature. |
  Barbershops–History–Juvenile literature.
Classification: LCC HD8039.B3 .H66 2020 | DDC 646.7/2409–dc23
LC record available at https://lccn.loc.gov/2019009057

Manufactured in the United States of America

CPSIA Compliance Information: Batch #CWPK20. For Further Information contact Rosen Publishing, New York, New York at 1-800-237-9932.

CONTENTS

The Barbershop

Have you ever tried to cut your own hair? It probably didn't go very well. Cutting hair is much harder than it looks! If you want a great haircut, you could visit your local barber at the barbershop.

What Is a Barber?

Barbers are trained to cut hair. They know how to shave and **groom** beards and mustaches. They have special tools to trim and shape hair into many styles. Most people who see the barber are men, but anyone who wants a haircut can visit the local barber.

Barber Surgeons

Many years ago in Europe, barbers often performed **surgery**. A barber might cut someone's hair and then cut out a rotten tooth! Doctors thought that cutting a sick person and making them bleed would help them get better. Barbers also did this service for people.

The Barber's Pole

The barber's pole is linked to barber history—and it's really gross! The red stands for blood. The blue stands for a person's **veins**. The white stands for **bandages**. Barbers used to hang their bandages outside in the wind to dry. They'd wrap around the pole.

More Than a Trim

Lots of people go to the barber for a trim, or a quick haircut. Barbers use tools called scissors and clippers to create different hairstyles. They sometimes add color to their customers' hair. They also wash, shave, and trim beards.

13

Get Comfy

People go to the barber because they want to look their best. But barbers want you to feel good, too. They help their customers get **comfortable**. They listen to them and make sure they're happy with their hairstyle before they leave.

First Barbers in America

In the early United States, people considered cutting hair to be **servants**' work. Most barbers were African American. Later, during the mid-1900s, **segregation** laws kept white people and black people separate in public. Barbershops became places where African Americans felt safe to meet and talk.

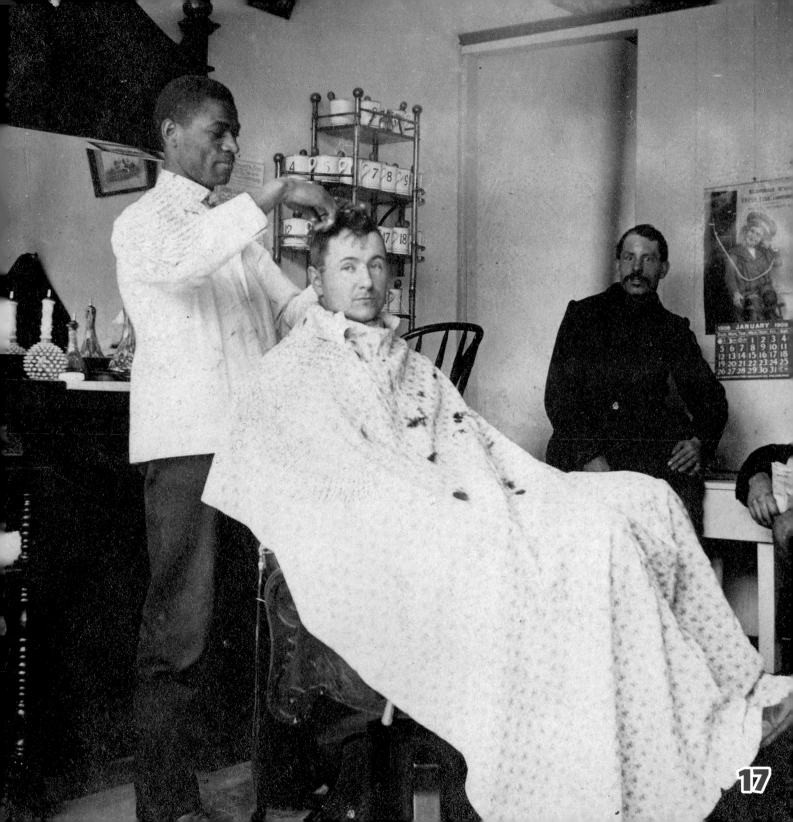

Barbershops Today

Today, many cities and towns still have local barbershops. They may be places where friends meet to chat and get a haircut. Barbershops are still important places in many African American communities. They still provide a place for people to meet and talk.

Barber Training

In most states, barbers must finish high school. Then, they take barbering classes. They have to pass a test and show their barbering skills to get a job. Barbers need to keep their customers happy, so they should be friendly and kind.

Looking Good, Feeling Good

Barbers aren't just good with a pair of scissors. They're artists who make new and exciting hairstyles. They're friends who listen to people talk about their day. Barbers are workers in our community that keep us looking good and also feeling good!

GLOSSARY

bandage: A strip of cloth used to cover a cut and stop bleeding.

comfortable: At ease.

groom: To make clean and neat.

segregation: The separation of people based on race.

servant: Someone who performs jobs for an employer.

surgery: A medical treatment in which a doctor cuts into someone's body.

vein: A tube in the body that carries blood to the heart.

INDEX

WEBSITES

Due to the changing nature of Internet links, PowerKids Press has developed an online list of websites related to the subject of this book. This site is updated regularly. Please use this link to access the list: www.powerkidslinks.com/HIOC/barbers